SIP THE STRAW

Sam Keck Scott & Woody Heffern

Illustrated by Nyoman Miasa

SocialMotion
PUBLISHING

Sip the Straw
Copyright © 2019 Sam Keck Scott and Woody Heffern

60% of the royalties from the sales of this book
go to Jr Ocean Guardians to fulfill its mission.
For more information, go to JrOceanGuardians.org.

Illustrations by Nyoman Miasa

Published by Social Motion Publishing,
the first and only publisher in the
United States dedicated to social-impact books.
SocialMotionPublishing.com

First print edition

ISBN: 978-0-578-41752-3

Produced in the United States of America

Four strangers became friends and came together,
from across the globe, to address an issue through a story.

Because a good story can change the world by changing a heart.

—The Sip Team

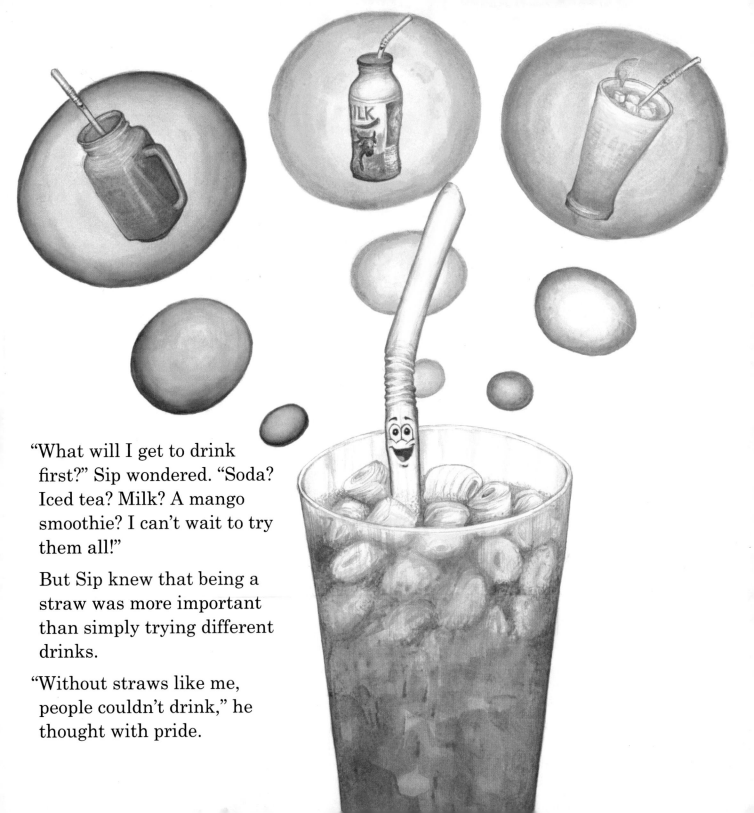

"What will I get to drink first?" Sip wondered. "Soda? Iced tea? Milk? A mango smoothie? I can't wait to try them all!"

But Sip knew that being a straw was more important than simply trying different drinks.

"Without straws like me, people couldn't drink," he thought with pride.

Sip watched as a large-handed man plucked his fellow straws from the box one by one.

He was next!

"There must be hundreds of thirsty people out there," he thought. "I bet they've been waiting a long time for us straws to arrive!"

Finally it was Sip's turn. The large-handed man picked him up and plunked him into a tall glass. It was filled with clear, frozen squares and a sweet brown liquid with tiny bubbles dancing on its surface.

Sip shivered from the cold, but he couldn't stop smiling.

"What is this drink?" he wondered.

Sip was whisked over to a table and placed in front of a woman reading a book. She didn't even look down before picking up the glass and bringing Sip to her mouth.

Sip's eyes were wide open in anticipation of his first drink.

Sip felt a most pleasant sensation as he was filled with sugary bubbles.

"Soda!"

It only took the woman three swallows to finish the entire thing.

The large-handed man grabbed the glass off the table and rushed Sip back to the kitchen.

"Wow, she must have been thirsty!" thought Sip. "I can't wait to find out what she'll order next!"

But then the strangest thing happened: The large-handed man grabbed Sip from the glass and dropped him into a trashcan!

"That silly man just threw me away!" Sip chuckled to himself, sure that the man would soon realize his mistake when the woman ordered her next drink and he was needed again.

But as Sip's eyes adjusted to the darkness he was startled to see that he wasn't the only straw in the can — there were at least twenty others mixed in with the rest of the garbage.

The large-handed man kept putting more and more trash on top of Sip and the other straws. When the bag was full, he tied the top of it shut and threw it out the back door of the restaurant.

"What are we doing in here?" Sip whispered to another straw.

"I don't know," the other straw replied, sounding worried.

After dark, a dog came along and tore the trash bag open. Sip spilled out onto the street with the rest of the trash.

Then the rain started.

It quickly became a downpour, and Sip got pulled by the water right into a storm drain.

Sip was in an underground pipe that sucked him away like it was the biggest straw in the world.

In the morning, he erupted out of the end of the pipe and flew through the air into the largest drink he had ever seen.

Sip was underwater with lots of trash and tree branches, but he soon drifted off and was all alone.

"What is this place?" he wondered.

It was bigger than anything he had ever imagined and tasted salty.

Three dolphins swam past Sip.

"Excuse me!" he shouted to them. "Can you help me, please?"

But the dolphins only glared at him and kept on swimming.

"Didn't they hear me?" Sip wondered, confused.

A huge sunfish rose silently from the depths towards Sip.

"Excuse me... sir? Do you know where I am?" Sip timidly asked th enormous fish.

"Sir?" the sunfish boomed, looking offended. "It's *miss*, thank you very much. Miss Mola, to be more specific. And you're in the ocean, little fella."

"The ocean?" yelled Sip. "But I'm a straw. I'm not supposed to be in the ocean!"

"You've got that right," Miss Mola replied, before flicking her giant fins and gliding away.

"Wait!" Sip yelled. "Where are you going?"

"The opposite direction from you," she said. "This is as close to the G.P.G.P as I'm willing to get."

"The G.P.G.P.?"

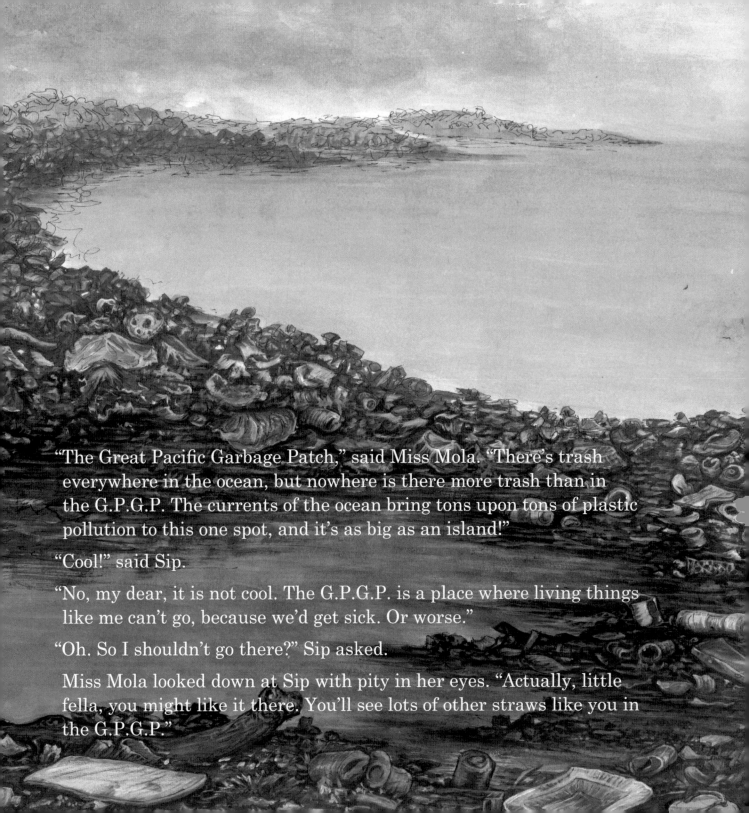

"The Great Pacific Garbage Patch," said Miss Mola. "There's trash everywhere in the ocean, but nowhere is there more trash than in the G.P.G.P. The currents of the ocean bring tons upon tons of plastic pollution to this one spot, and it's as big as an island!"

"Cool!" said Sip.

"No, my dear, it is not cool. The G.P.G.P. is a place where living things like me can't go, because we'd get sick. Or worse."

"Oh. So I shouldn't go there?" Sip asked.

Miss Mola looked down at Sip with pity in her eyes. "Actually, little fella, you might like it there. You'll see lots of other straws like you in the G.P.G.P."

Sip didn't want to leave Miss Mola, but he felt himself being pulled by an invisible force in the opposite direction from where she was swimming.

"Good luck!" Miss Mola shouted.

"Goodbye, Miss Mola!"

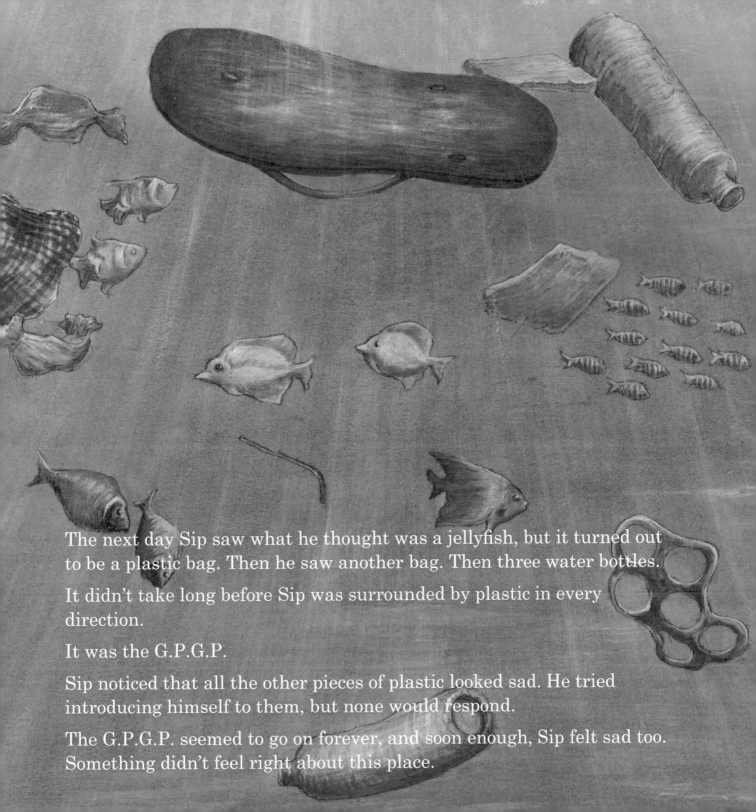

The next day Sip saw what he thought was a jellyfish, but it turned out to be a plastic bag. Then he saw another bag. Then three water bottles.

It didn't take long before Sip was surrounded by plastic in every direction.

It was the G.P.G.P.

Sip noticed that all the other pieces of plastic looked sad. He tried introducing himself to them, but none would respond.

The G.P.G.P. seemed to go on forever, and soon enough, Sip felt sad too. Something didn't feel right about this place.

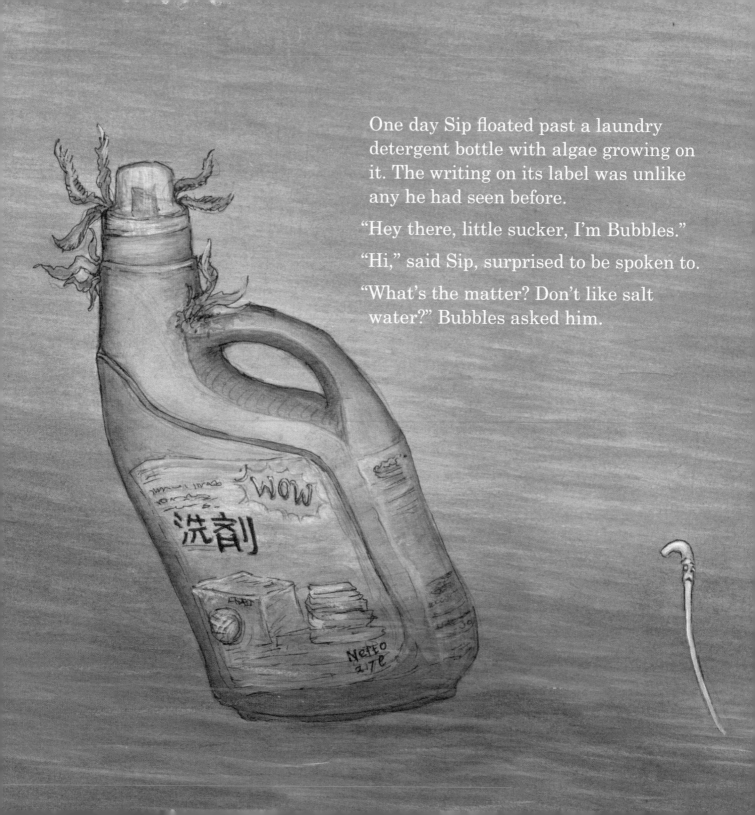

One day Sip floated past a laundry detergent bottle with algae growing on it. The writing on its label was unlike any he had seen before.

"Hey there, little sucker, I'm Bubbles."

"Hi," said Sip, surprised to be spoken to.

"What's the matter? Don't like salt water?" Bubbles asked him.

"I'm just sad, and a little confused," said Sip. "I thought being a straw would be a noble life. But now I just feel like a... a piece of trash."

"Welcome to the club!" Bubbles said with a bubbly laugh. "You *are* a piece of trash! Everyone here is."

"But how can I be a piece of trash?" Sip asked. "People can't drink without straws. What could be more important than helping people drink?"

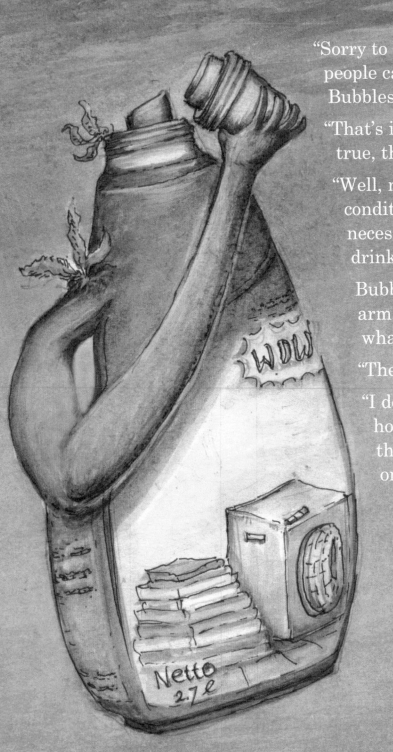

"Sorry to break it to you, little sucker, but most people can drink just fine without straws," Bubbles told his new friend.

"That's impossible!" shouted Sip. "If that were true, then why would I exist at all?"

"Well, many people do have physical conditions that make using a straw necessary. But for most people, they can drink just like this."

Bubbles stretched his handle out like an arm. Then he used his own cap to show Sip what drinking without a straw looks like.

"Then why do people use straws?"

"I don't know, Sip. But if they could see how many of you end up here, I bet they'd think twice about ever using one again."

Sip was crushed. His entire existence was a waste. Not only was being a straw not noble like he had imagined, but he was ruining the home of animals like Miss Mola.

"Hey, it's not your fault," said Bubbles. "Nobody asked you if you wanted to be used one time before getting thrown away, now did they?"

Once Sip had stopped crying, he asked Bubbles: "So if we're both just trash, how come you seem so happy?"

"Because I still have a dream," Bubbles answered.

"What dream?"

"A dream of becoming a mooring buoy!" Bubbles declared with pride.

"What's that?"

"Sometimes bottles like me are used as buoys to tie boats to," Bubbles began. "The buoy has a rope attached to it that's tied to something heavy on the bottom, like a concrete block. Some are made to protect coral reefs so anchors won't be dropped on them. That's the kind I want to be."

"That sounds wonderful," said Sip.

"Doesn't it? The best thing that can happen to plastic like us is being given a new purpose," said Bubbles. "I've been a piece of trash for twelve years now. I've still got a few hundred years to go before I'll start decomposing, so I'd sure like to make myself useful in the meantime."

Sip began to wonder how he could become useful someday...

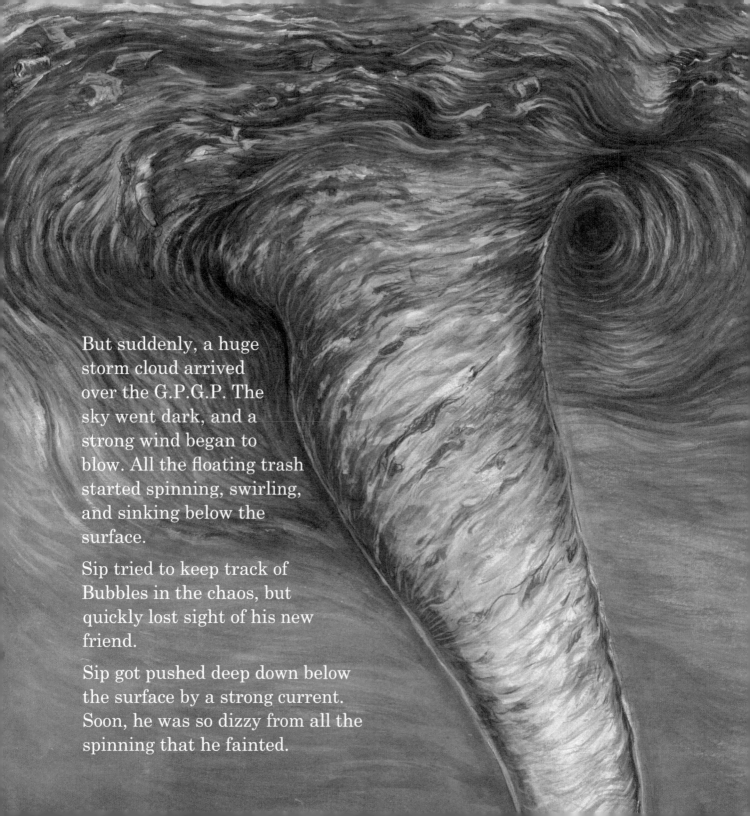

But suddenly, a huge storm cloud arrived over the G.P.G.P. The sky went dark, and a strong wind began to blow. All the floating trash started spinning, swirling, and sinking below the surface.

Sip tried to keep track of Bubbles in the chaos, but quickly lost sight of his new friend.

Sip got pushed deep down below the surface by a strong current. Soon, he was so dizzy from all the spinning that he fainted.

When Sip woke up, he felt something funny beneath him.

"I'm not floating!" he realized.

He was lying in the sand.

Just as Sip began to look around to see where he was, a small hand picked him up.

The young girl who found Sip carried him to a beautiful sandcastle on the beach.

"You're just what I was looking for," she said, smiling down at Sip.

The girl placed Sip carefully on the very top of her sandcastle, and tied some dry seaweed to him.

"Now my castle has a flag!" she said proudly.

Sip tried to talk to the girl, but she couldn't hear him.

Soon, however, a soft breeze began to blow. As the wind ran across the hole at the top of Sip's head, it made a small whistling sound. Using the whistling wind, Sip tried to speak to the girl again.

"Can you hear me?" he said.

"Who said that?"

"It's me, Sip the straw, I mean… flagpole."

The girl looked puzzled and brought her ear closer to Sip.

"Listen, there's something very important that I need your help with," said Sip.

"What is it?" said the girl.

"I need you to tell every person you know to stop drinking out of plastic straws like me."

"But why?" asked the girl.

"Because we're polluting the oceans, and covering the beaches, and filling the landfills, and it needs to stop. Help me be the last straw you ever find on the beach."

"I promise. Okay, I'll do it!," she said with a smile.

Just then, the girl's parents arrived.

"Time to go, honey," they said.

Sip watched with sadness as his new friend got up and began walking away down the beach with her parents.

"Wait!" the girl suddenly shouted.

She turned around and ran back to her sandcastle and pulled Sip from the top of it.

"Mom, can you help me put this around my wrist?"

"No, dear, that's garbage. Just leave it where you found it."

"It won't be garbage anymore if you help me make it into a bracelet."

"Oh, all right," the mother said, placing one end of Sip into the other around her daughter's wrist.

"First a flagpole, and now a bracelet," thought Sip. "Today is my lucky day!"

With the wind in his face, Sip looked out at the big blue ocean and thought about his friend, Miss Mola. He understood now that her home was not meant for straws and plastic bags, but only for the living creatures of the sea.

Sip then thought of Bubbles and hoped that he was getting closer to his dream of becoming a mooring buoy.

"Mom? Dad?" the little girl spoke from the backseat.

"Yes, dear?"

"Can we have a new rule in this family?"

"A new rule?"

"Yes. From now on, none of us will ever drink out of a plastic straw again!"

The girl looked down at Sip and winked, and Sip smiled.

Perhaps his life would be noble after all.

The End

People use and throw away millions of plastic straws per day in the United States alone, many of which end up in our oceans and harm animals. You can help put an end to this wasteful practice by pledging to stop using plastic straws today, and setting an example for others to do the same.

One easy way to do this is to buy a straw you don't throw away. These are often made out of bamboo, stainless steel, or recycled aluminum, which is much better for our environment.

Also, when you order a drink at a restaurant, tell your server: "No straw, please." And suggest they put up signs that read: "Straws by request only."

Together, we can help spread this important message so other straws like Sip don't end up in our oceans.

From left to right: Woody, Nyoman, and Sam
working on the book in Bali, Indonesia.

**"Special thanks to Yves De Leeneer for completing the team
and to our friends around the planet."**

About the Authors and Illustrator

Woody Heffern was born in the United States and grew up in a large family, living most of his life overseas. His love for the water started at age six when he and his friends went fishing for his birthday party. He was instantly hooked. He continues to find ways to spend his free time on and under water. As a certified Rescue Diver he has trained and promised to assist others in need. Right now, it is our rivers and oceans that need help. Sip and this story are the first product of that promise. There will be others.

Sam Keck Scott is a writer, biologist, conservationist, and avid adventurer. He is a regularly featured author on the National Geographic Society Blog, a Writing By Writers Fellow, and a winner of the John Gardner Memorial Prize. Sam recently spent three months sailing through remote Indonesia and saw firsthand the devastating effects that single-use plastics are having on our planet's oceans and beaches, and became determined to help. When not exploring some far-flung land or sea, Sam lives in an airstream trailer tucked between two dilapidated chicken coops in rural Sonoma County, in Northern California.

Nyoman Miasa was born and raised in Ubud, Bali, where he still lives today. He is a painter, fisherman, husband, and the father of two daughters. This is his first book of illustrations.

60 percent of the royalties from sales of this book go to the nonprofit organization Jr Ocean Guardians.

Plastic straws are one of the main ocean plastic polluters—help change that! One big goal of Jr Ocean Guardians is to make people aware of the millions of plastic straws that are used once and then thrown away. The organization encourages you to refuse plastic straws and ask the businesses you visit, like restaurants, hotels, and airlines, to adopt a policy of "straws available on request."

Plastic straws are medically and physically necessary for some people. Jr Ocean Guardians does not condone shaming of those who rely on straws.

JrOceanGuardians.org

Made in the USA
San Bernardino, CA
10 January 2020

62990232R00022